OTHER BOOKS
BY THICH NHAT HANH

HOW TO LIVE WHEN A LOVED ONE DIES

Healing Meditations for Grief and Loss

THICH NHAT HANH

PARALLAX PRESS
BERKELEY, CALIFORNIA

PARALLAX PRESS
2236B SIXTH STREET
BERKELEY, CA 94710
PARALLAX.ORG

Parallax Press is the publishing division of
Plum Village Community of Engaged Buddhism

Cover and text design by Katie Eberle

Typeset by Maureen Forys, Happenstance Type-O-Rama

All poems in this book are by Thich Nhat Hanh

The material in this book comes from previously
published books and unpublished Dharma
talks by Thich Nhat Hanh
Edited and with complementary practices
by Sister Tri Nghiem
and the editors of Parallax Press

Printed in the United States of America
on recycled paper

LCCN 2021011340 | ISBN 9781946764805 |
ISBN 9781946764812 (e-book)

3 4 5 6 7 / 27 26 25 24 23

ONENESS

The moment I die,
I will try to come back to you
as quickly as possible.
I promise it will not take long.
Isn't it true
I am already with you,
as I die each moment?
I come back to you
in every moment.
Just look,
feel my presence.
If you want to cry,
please cry.
And know
that I will cry with you.
The tears you shed will heal us both.
Your tears are mine.

EDITORS' NOTE

Here are some of Zen Master Thich Nhat Hanh's most insightful teachings on grief and loss, together with self-care meditations and practices in the Plum Village tradition compiled by the editors. We hope these meditations and practices will help you find relief, comfort, and healing in the face of grief and loss, and help you reconnect with yourself, your loved one, and all of life.

CONTENTS

GRIEF

Our loved ones are in us and we are in them.
When a loved one dies, a part of us also dies.

Sometimes we think that our loss is so great that we will never be able to be happy again.

When we lose a loved one, our heart is filled
with a deep suffering that we cannot express.
But we can express our pain in tears. We can
cry. When you cry, you feel better.

Men can cry, too. I wanted to cry when I
saw someone else crying. It is human nature to
cry. To be able to cry brings comfort, relief, and
healing.

If you want to cry, please cry.
And know that I will cry with you.
The tears you shed will heal us both.
Your tears are mine.

I stamped my feet and
cried the moment mother
died.
That morning was a beautiful rosy
morning, but at midnight the wind blew
hard.

LIKE A TREE
IN A STORM

When a painful emotion comes up, stop whatever you are doing and take care of it right away. Bring your attention home to what is happening in your body. The practice is simple.

Put your hand on your belly and feel the movement of your breathing. Bring all your awareness down from your head to your navel and stop thinking about what has upset you. In a storm, the leaves and branches at the top of the tree thrash about wildly. The tree looks so fragile and vulnerable, as though it could break at any moment. But when you bring your attention down to the trunk of the tree, you see the trunk is very calm and still. You are no longer afraid because you realize that the tree is strong and stable, that it is deeply rooted in the soil and can withstand the storm.

SELF-CARE
BELLY BREATHING

A strong emotion is like a storm, but if we know how to practice, we can survive the storm. When we are caught in a storm of strong emotions, we need to identify what is causing our emotional response and gently disengage ourselves from it straight away. Whether it is a thought, an image, a sound, a smell, a touch, or a person speaking, we turn our attention away from it for a moment and bring all our attention back to our breathing. If we continue to pay attention to or think about what is causing us to suffer, it will only increase our strong emotions.

So, we practice deep belly breathing. Whether standing, sitting, or lying down, we become aware of our breathing. If our breathing is rapid and shallow, we notice it, and shift our attention from our throat and chest down to our belly and focus on the rising and falling of our abdomen.

The practice is simple:

Breathing in, I am aware of my abdomen rising.
Breathing out, I am aware of my abdomen falling.

Gradually the storm will subside, our breathing and our heart will calm down, and we will feel more at peace.

LISTEN TO YOURSELF

When you are suffering greatly, if you have suffered a profound loss, you need people who are able to just sit and listen to you with compassion. But what is even more important is that we can listen to ourselves with compassion. To do this, we need to learn the art of deep listening. We stop whatever we're doing and come home to ourselves. We look deeply to recognize and name our suffering and embrace it tenderly. Listening deeply to our own suffering is an act of self-compassion.

SELF-CARE
CONSCIOUS BREATHING

When we lose a loved one, especially if it was sudden and unexpected, we may feel like we have lost the ground under our feet. It takes our breath away.

The first thing to do is to regain our footing. The practice of conscious breathing can help us come back to the present moment and come back into the body.

How to calm a racing heart and erratic breathing? It is actually very simple—we bring all our awareness back to our breath and focus exclusively on our breathing. We stop thinking about anything else and follow the breath as it moves in and out of the body.

° ° °

Continue to follow your breathing. Feel the cool air entering your body and notice that it is warmer when it leaves. We become aware of which parts of the body are moving as we breathe in and out, and we focus on the rising and falling of the abdomen.

When we maintain awareness of our breath, our breathing naturally becomes lighter, calmer, and more peaceful. Gradually the storm subsides and our mind and body calm down.

° ° °

Your breath is your life raft in a stormy ocean, the anchor keeping you in your body. Follow your breath and notice what is happening in your body. Feel your abdomen rising and falling. When we are very upset, our breathing may be fast and shallow and our chest may heave. Just focus on these bodily sensations. Become aware of any constrictions in the body, any tightness or pain, and do your best to breathe into those places and release the tension. Keep your awareness on your bodily sensations and the flow of your breathing. Do not try to change or force anything; just become aware of what is happening. Your breathing will naturally start to calm down, and your mind and body will begin to relax and calm down as well.

Wherever we are, we can practice conscious breathing, whether we're sitting, walking, standing, or lying down. Just following your breathing can already bring a lot of peace and relief. Whenever we become overwhelmed with grief, despair, or sorrow, our breathing is the stable, solid ground that we can take refuge in.

o o o

To help us stay focused on our breathing, with each in and out breath we may like to say silently,

Breathing in, I know I'm breathing in.
Breathing out, I know I'm breathing out.

In.
Out.

Gently follow your in- and out-breath with concentration and awareness all the way through, from the beginning to the end. Don't force or try to change your breathing, just observe and follow it. If your mind wanders off, gently invite it back to follow your breathing again. Our breathing will naturally calm down and become a little slower and deeper.

Breathing in, I follow my in-breath all the way through.
Breathing out, I follow my out-breath all the way through.

Following my in-breath,
Following my out-breath.

Maintain your concentration as long as possible. Awareness of your breathing brings your mind back to your body, and back to the present moment. Become aware of your body; remember that you have a body. Release any tension—in your face, your shoulders, your diaphragm—and allow your body to relax. This is the first step to restoring wellness.

○ ○ ○

Put your hands on your abdomen and feel it rising and falling. Now, as you follow your breath, you can say to yourself,

Breathing in, I become aware of my whole body.
Breathing out, I relax all the muscles in my body.

Aware of body.
Relaxing body.

Breathing in, I calm my body
Breathing out, I smile

Calm,
Smile.

A gentle half smile will release all the muscles in your face. If we can smile to our suffering, we can already feel some relief. We do not need to wait until we feel like smiling in order to smile. Sometimes we feel good and we smile, but sometimes we smile and this makes us feel better. Neuroscience research now shows this is so. A smile says, "This is not the end of the world, even if it feels like it."

If it is easier, you may like to simply repeat short words for each in- and out-breath, anchoring your awareness with these key words or other words of your choosing:

In, out.
Deep, slow.
Calm, ease.
Smile, release.

Keep breathing with these words. Notice that your out-breath is often longer than your in-breath. Savor the pause at the end of your out-breath; relax and allow all the tension in your body to slowly dissipate.

WHEN IT'S HARD TO SIT STILL

When we find it difficult to come back to our breathing and calm our strong emotions, going out for a walk can help.

We walk in mindfulness, aware of what is happening inside us and around us. In this way we come home and take refuge in the present moment and in nature. As we walk, we let go of our regrets about the past and our worries about the future and remain fully established in the here and now. We let ourselves be nourished by the earth, the sky, the fresh air, and the sun. We walk and allow our mind to rest. We dwell peacefully in the here and now and let nature heal us.

Walk as a free person. Bring your awareness down to your feet, don't stay in your head. Feel the contact between your foot and the ground.

WALKING MEDITATION

Walking meditation brings body and mind together and restores peace. We bring our mind back to the present moment with each step. Walk in peace, with self-sovereignty. Let go of sadness and worries, and release them to the earth. When these feelings resurface, just say "Hello" and "Goodbye" to them. Don't force yourself not to feel sad. Just recognize the feeling and gently let it go. Come back to your breathing and your steps.

In walking meditation, we combine our breathing with our steps. While breathing in, we may take two or three steps. As we breathe out, we may want to take a few more steps. Let the rhythm of your breathing and walking be natural, whatever fits your own breath. We can use words to help us coordinate our steps and our breath. As we breathe in and take two

or three steps, we can say, "I have arrived."
As we breathe out, we can say, "I am home."
With every step, we really arrive; we're really
at home. We arrive in the present moment; we
don't lose ourselves in the past or the future.
We feel safe, peaceful, and at ease when we are
fully established in the present moment. You
can also say, "With every step, I return to my
source." We can use whatever words or sen-
tences we like.

When we do walking meditation, our body
and mind are united. Walking meditation is a
wonderful practice that can help us to return to
ourselves and find healing from Mother Earth.

SELF-CARE
FINDING RELIEF IN WALKING
MEDITATION

In times of stress and grief, walking meditation is a wonderful way to reestablish peace and calm in the body and mind. Spending time walking in nature every day helps reconnect us with our body, the earth, and the wonders of life. Nature has the capacity to embrace our pain and transform it.

We do not walk with the aim of getting anywhere, we just walk for the pure joy of walking. We enjoy every step we make, savoring our breath and releasing our pain and sorrow to the earth. Every step brings us home to the present moment, the only place where life is possible.

We become aware of our breathing and the contact of our feet on the earth. We feel the warmth of the sun on our face and the breeze on our skin. We become aware of the sounds of the birds, and the fragrance of the trees and flowers around us. We enjoy every step; with each step we make an imprint of peace on the earth. We can practice in a park or some other beautiful, quiet place. This nourishes our spirit, strengthens our mindfulness, and helps us heal.

o o o

When we walk, we can take the hand of our loved one who has passed away and walk with them. Our legs are their legs, and our eyes are their eyes. When we see something beautiful—the blue sky, a brilliant sunset, a majestic tree, or an animal—we can stop walking to allow this sight to penetrate our consciousness and nourish us deeply. We allow this beauty not only to nourish us, but to nourish our loved one in us. We enjoy everything, not only for ourselves but also for our loved one who has died.

∘ ∘ ∘

Make gentle steps; imagine you are kissing the earth with your feet. Bring your awareness down to the soles of your feet and feel the contact of your feet and the earth. Let the earth support you. Really arrive with each step. If you have not arrived yet, stop walking until you are fully present. Coordinate your breath and your steps so there is communication between them. You may like to count your steps as you breathe—depending on the length of your breath—two or three steps for an in-breath and three or four steps for an out-breath. *"One, two; one, two, three" or "In, in; out, out, out."*

Say a small poem to help you focus. Depending on the pace of your steps and your breathing, one word or phrase can accompany one step.

I have arrived, I am home
In the here and in the now

Or, more simply:

Arrived, arrived,
Home, home, home.

SANCTUARY IN THE ISLAND OF SELF

When life seems like a turbulent ocean, we can remember we have an island of peace inside. Everything is impermanent—coming and going, love and hate, birth and death—everything is always in the process of changing. Dwelling in the island of self, you are safe. Take refuge in your own island.

Breathing in, make two steps and say, "Taking refuge." Breathing out, make two or three steps and say, "In the island of self."

Breathing in, I go back to the island within myself.
There are beautiful trees within the island.
There are clear streams of water, there are birds,
      sunshine, and fresh air.
Breathing out, I feel safe.
I enjoy going back to my island.

WE ALL NEED HELP SOMETIMES

There are times when our suffering is so great, it needs more than just one person to hold it.

When suffering threatens to overwhelm us, we can call on the support of others. A group of people who practice mindfulness together can provide such support. The collective energy of mindfulness generated by the group has the power to hold us and our pain. The practice of deep listening and loving speech can offer relief. Practicing sitting and walking meditation together, touching the earth with our feet, can be very healing.

We allow the collective energy of mindfulness to recognize and embrace our pain. It can be a heavy burden to carry our pain alone, so we entrust it to the group. "Dear friends, here is my pain, here is my sorrow, here is my despair.

Please help me acknowledge it. Please hold it for me."

We become a drop of water flowing in the river of awakened energy and we feel much better. The collective energy of mindfulness is transformative, powerful, and healing.

PEACE IS EVERY STEP

Peace is all around us, in the world and in nature. Peace is also within us, in our bodies and mind. The act of walking waters the seeds of peace that are already there inside us. Our mindful steps help us cultivate the habit of touching peace in each moment.

The mind can go in a thousand directions.
But on this beautiful path, I walk in peace.
With each step, a gentle wind blows.
With each step, a flower blooms.

SURVIVING OUR
STRONG EMOTIONS

Feelings come and go like clouds in a windy sky.
Conscious breathing is my anchor.

TAKE ONE
BREATH

Healing begins when we breathe in. There is no way to healing; healing is the way. When we breathe in mindfully, we bring our mind home to our body, uniting body and mind, and the mind stops racing. Sometimes just one breath is all it takes.

WE ARE MORE THAN OUR EMOTIONS

Right now, you may find life unbearable. Yet everything is impermanent. Our emotions are impermanent; they come and they go. This insight can save your life. An emotion comes, stays for a while, and then it goes. This is the nature of all phenomena.

You are so much more than your emotions. You are your body, your feelings, your perceptions, mental formations, and consciousness. You are your actions of body, speech, and mind. You are your aspirations, your capacity to love and understand; and you are connected with all of life. The territory of your being is infinite.

Focusing our attention on the rising and falling of our abdomen as we breathe deeply, our emotions will no longer overwhelm us or push us to do something destructive. When you survive a strong emotion once, you will have confidence that you can do the same again the next time.

GOING HOME TO NATURE

The earth is our home. She is our true mother. In times of grief and loss, we can return to the earth who gave birth to us. The earth can embrace us and all our sadness and despair. She is always ready to receive you. Her arms are always open for you. Nature invites you to dive into her lap. Fall into her loving embrace and surrender yourself; release your suffering. The relief that we seek is right under our feet, and all around us. Each mindful step on the earth can heal us.

TAKING REFUGE
IN THE EARTH

When we are feeling fragile and unstable, we can come home and take refuge in the earth. With each step we feel her solidity beneath our feet. When we're truly in touch with the Earth, we can feel her endless compassion, her stability and non-discrimination, and her healing embrace. We go back to the Earth and surrender ourselves to her.

When we know how to go back to Mother Earth, we feel nourished, and regain our peace. Mother Earth has the power to nourish us, hold our suffering, and heal us. When we reconnect with her solidity beneath our feet, we can experience deep healing. We rejoice in her majesty, in her high mountain peaks and lakes, in the vast blue sky, winding rivers, and deep oceans. The sun embraces and caresses us every day, lighting up our days, months, and years, bringing light into our lives.

When we can come back to ourselves and take refuge in our inner island, we become a home for ourselves, and we become a refuge for others at the same time. Walking with one hundred percent of your body and mind can free you from anger, fear, and despair. Each step can express your love for the Earth and for yourself.

While walking, you can say,

With each step,
I come home to the Earth.
With each step,
I return to my source.
With each step,
I take refuge in Mother Earth.

CALMING OUR PAINFUL FEELINGS

In the same way that we practice calming our breathing and our body, we can practice calming our feelings. Come back to your breathing; recognize, embrace, and calm your painful feelings of sadness, grief, and loss. That is the practice: not to push them away but to identify, name, and embrace our feelings tenderly, as a mother would embrace her crying baby.

Identifying and naming our painful feelings reduces their power over us. It is important to know what we are feeling. Our peaceful breathing and compassionate embrace will calm these strong emotions and allow them to transform naturally.

If we are lucky enough to be in an environment where there are other people practicing mindfulness, we can benefit from the collective energy of mindfulness.

What is stopping us from feeling joy in the present moment? What is the true nature of our suffering? We can learn to call all our feelings by their true names.

SELF-CARE
EMBRACING AND CALMING OUR
PAINFUL FEELINGS

Find a quiet place to sit and follow your breathing. Use these prompts to help guide you. Each line of the guided meditation below accompanies your in-breath or out-breath respectively. After each line, you may like to close your eyes and enjoy a few in-breaths and out-breaths, holding the key words in your heart. The first key phrase accompanies the in-breath, the second key phrase accompanies the out-breath.

Aware of the state of my mind,
I breathe in.
Smiling to the state of my mind,
I breathe out.
Aware of mind.
Smiling.

Experiencing the pain of grief in me,
I breathe in.
Smiling to the pain of grief,
I breathe out.
Experiencing grief
Smiling.

Experiencing the deep sadness
in me, I breathe in.
Smiling to the feeling of sadness,
I breathe out.
Experiencing profound sadness.
Smiling.

If you encounter resistance, keep going anyway. It may seem impossible to smile, but even the idea of smiling can help us feel relief.

Embracing my difficult feelings,
I breathe in.
Smiling to my difficult feelings,
I breathe out.
Embracing feelings.
Smiling.

Soothing my difficult feelings,
I breathe in.
Feeling release,
I breathe out.
Soothing
Release.

Taking refuge in the present moment,
I breathe in.
Smiling and accepting,
I breathe out.
Present moment.
Smiling and accepting.

When you are overwhelmed by strong emotions like grief, sorrow, anger, or despair, you can practice with guided meditations like these to help you calm down and find relief. When we can recognize, name, and embrace our difficult emotions, they calm down naturally, and give space to something else.

WHEN WE ARE OVERWHELMED BY GRIEF

If we let the suffering come up and take over our mind, we can quickly be overwhelmed by it. So, we invite another energy to come up at the same time, the energy of mindfulness.

With the energy of mindfulness, we can recognize our pain and embrace it tenderly like a mother whose baby is crying. When a baby cries, the mother stops everything she is doing and holds the baby tenderly in her arms. The energy of the mother will penetrate into the baby and the baby will feel relief.

The function of mindfulness is, first, to recognize the suffering that is there and then to take care of the suffering by identifying and embracing it. It is important that we are able to name what we are feeling, to identify what is making us suffer so that transformation, peace, and joy can be possible.

When we can embrace our sorrow and pain, our anger and fear, with the energy of mindfulness, we'll be able to recognize the roots of our suffering. And we'll be able to recognize the suffering in the people we love as well.

THE MIRACLE OF MINDFULNESS

Mindfulness can heal us and transform our grief and sorrow. It is the energy that helps us know what is happening in the present moment, within us and around us. It is possible to change our life with the practice of mindful breathing, sitting, and walking. If we can manage to be mindful while doing these basic things, then we'll more easily be able to handle our painful feelings and emotions when they arise.

FIRST, NOURISH YOURSELF

Practicing mindfulness, we start to become more aware of our pain; however, we may not yet be strong enough to transform it. To have the strength to fully face and embrace our pain, it is important that we stay in touch with the many wonderful and refreshing things that are both inside us and all around us—the trees, the blue sky, the eyes of a child, the setting sun. We need to have a solid foundation in order to be strong enough to bear our suffering. When we are calm and stable, when we have cultivated enough peace and joy, then we can bear to look at our suffering. Just as a surgeon may judge a patient too weak to undergo surgery and recommend that the patient first get some rest and nourishment to build up their strength so they can survive the surgery, we need to strengthen our foundation of joy and happiness before focusing on our suffering.

NURTURING OUR POSITIVE EMOTIONS

The mind is like the earth. Seeds of all kinds lie deep in the earth. We all have many kinds of seeds lying in the depths of our consciousness— wholesome and unwholesome seeds. When the seeds are watered, they sprout and manifest in mind consciousness as mental formations. In our own consciousness there is heaven but there is also hell. We are all capable of being happy, compassionate, and understanding but if we focus only on the negative things within us, especially our sadness, our pain, and suffering, this will water our seeds of sorrow, despair, and hopelessness. These seeds will then sprout and grow big and strong, and become stronger at the base. So, what we choose to water is important. We need positive nourishment in order to grow our happiness. Practicing appropriate attention, we are selective in what we water. We water the

41

wholesome qualities in us by getting in touch with what is positive, within us and around us. This is how we touch the wonders of life that are always available to us.

One way of taking care of our suffering is to invite a seed of the opposite nature to come up. Nothing exists without its opposite. So if you have seeds of despair, you also have seeds of hope. If you have seeds of depression, you also have the seeds of joy and vitality.

When a negative seed like despair is watered, we can invite the seed of mindfulness to come up and embrace it, to help us recognize what we are feeling. If we feel lonely, we know we are feeling lonely. We can name it. Naming our feelings has an immediate impact on them, weakening the power of the negative seeds and strengthening the positive seeds at the base. Everyone has the seed of compassion. If you practice mindfulness of compassion every day, the seed of compassion in you will become strong and will become a powerful source of energy. The more we cultivate peace, joy, and happiness within us, our sadness and despair will naturally decrease.

We don't have to fight or push anything down; we just try to selectively water the good seeds and refrain from watering the negative seeds. This doesn't mean we ignore our suffering; it just means that we allow the positive seeds that are naturally there to receive attention and nourishment so they can sprout and grow and bring forth beautiful flowers.

STOPPING AND LOOKING DEEPLY

When we are overwhelmed by our suffering, the first thing to do is to stop what we are doing, bring our attention to our breathing and follow it with our awareness. Don't try to ignore or repress uncomfortable emotions.

> *Breathing in, I know I am breathing in*
> *Breathing out, I know I am breathing out.*

Follow your breathing until you start to calm down.

> *Breathing in, I know I am suffering.*
> *Breathing out, I say hello to my suffering.*

This is the way to practice stopping and looking deeply, the two wings of meditation. We stop everything and come back to our breathing so we can look deeply to recognize and take care of what is there.

SELF-CARE
STOPPING TO REST

To release some of the pain and tension in the body and mind, we can stop for a few moments at regular intervals throughout the day, no matter how busy our day is or how good or bad we are feeling. We can try to take a few seconds or a few minutes to stop—to breathe, to rest, to relax, and to heal. This will help prevent stress and tension from accumulating in our body and mind and will allow the body to restore itself.

When we stop and come back to our body, we are able to get in touch with what is positive. We can touch the wonders of life that are available to us in every instant. We feel peaceful and can see things with more clarity. When we stop, we can touch peace and joy, and smile again.

The body and mind are two sides of one reality. When our mind is too tense and filled with many worries, it affects our body. So we practice stopping—we stop running and with every breath we take and every step we make, we bring our mind back to our body and the present moment. Walk so that you enjoy every step, *really* enjoy every step, and let go of your sadness, worries, and anxiety. When these feelings reappear, just say "Hello" and "Goodbye." We don't need to force ourselves, or

45

struggle or feel bad. We just recognize the feelings and let them go, gently. Each time one of these painful feelings comes back, we just wave and say hello and goodbye again. "Hello my sadness, my despair. I know you are there. Goodbye my sadness, my despair." Slowly we become more relaxed, and over time healing takes place.

NO MUD, NO LOTUS

Love and understanding are the lotuses that bloom from the mud of suffering. Without the mud, there is no lotus flower. The lotus needs mud to grow. Understanding and compassion are possible only when we've come in touch with suffering.

We know that suffering plays an important role in generating understanding and love. So we do not run away from suffering, instead we embrace it, and look deeply into our suffering in order to understand it. If we can understand, then we can love. And when we have understanding and love, we suffer less.

SELF-CARE
SITTING MEDITATION
FOR HEALING

We all need a quiet place to retreat to and simply be. But especially in times of crisis or turmoil, we need a safe haven where we can sit and follow our breathing. Find or create a quiet place in your home where you can sit in peace and not be disturbed. You might like to set up a little altar or shrine, with flowers, incense, and a candle to help create a meditative and peaceful atmosphere. Your space should be a welcoming haven with soothing images, scents, and sounds. Come back to this quiet place whenever you need it.

Sitting meditation is not difficult. It is not hard labor. Many people may think sitting meditation is for the spiritually adept or for people who are supple in their bodies, but in fact there is nothing extraordinary about sitting meditation. Anyone can do it. All you need to do is find a quiet place and sit down.

Meditation is the art of stopping our racing mind and looking deeply into things. Sitting meditation is a quick and effective way to practice stopping. We stop speaking and moving and allow our body and mind to calm down. It only takes a few minutes, not long at all. We don't allow ourselves to be carried away by our regrets about the past or worries about the future. We come back to the present moment, where we are safe and where we can touch true peace. Life is available to us only in the present moment, and if we are not present, we miss out on life.

Stopping and sitting, following our breathing, is the way home. When we have brought our mind back to our body and established peace and calm, we find relief. When we are calm, things look different; we can see everything more clearly.

Imagine a glass of freshly pressed apple juice—at first it is very cloudy and we cannot see through it; but if we leave it to stand for a while, the pulp settles and the juice becomes clear. After a while of "sitting meditation," the juice looks like water—completely transparent. The same thing happens to our mind when we sit and follow our breathing—everything settles and calms down, and we gain more clarity. We see things in a different light. Looking deeply with mindfulness and concentration gives rise to insight. And with insight comes transformation and healing.

HOW TO SIT

You can either sit on the ground or sit on a chair. Sitting on the floor can help ground us and get our mind out of our head and back into the body. Sit cross-legged on a cushion or in the Japanese style using a small bench or a firm cushion between your heels for support.

Find a comfortable position, with your back upright but not rigid, your shoulders relaxed and your hands resting gently in your lap. Sit on the front edge of the cushion or chair so your spine is straight and relaxed. If your legs are crossed, make sure both knees are touching the floor so that your posture is stable and you do not need to make any effort to stay upright. If you are sitting on a chair, be sure your feet are flat on the floor or supported by a cushion or footrest.

Bring your awareness to your in-breath and out-breath. Your breathing will naturally become deeper, slower and more peaceful. It should feel very pleasant. Simply sitting and calming our body can bring a feeling of ease and well-being. Sit solely for the joy and nourishment of sitting. Let go of your thinking and just follow your breathing.

Now bring your awareness to your body, relaxing your body and releasing any tension you may be holding. Breathing mindfully brings your mind home to your body.

Your body is a miracle. When you can touch the wonder of your body, healing begins straight away. When you unite body and mind in the present moment, you touch true peace.

Sitting for the sake of sitting is an act of compassion we offer ourselves.

SELF-CARE
SEEING YOUR LOVED ONE
WITHIN YOU

When someone we love passes away, we may suddenly feel abandoned or alone and may believe that we have lost them forever. We may experience anguish and feel disconnected from them. However, when we reconnect with ourselves, we reconnect with our loved one, with our ancestors, and with the whole stream of life. When we come home to ourselves, we can touch our loved one within us.

Our parents are our closest ancestors. We know that, genetically speaking, all our ancestors are still alive in each of our cells. They have not died. But not only do we carry their genes, we also carry all their thoughts, beliefs, experiences, and aspirations within us. We carry their actions of body, speech, and mind into the future. You cannot take your loved one out of you, just as you cannot take your father or your mother out of you, even if you wanted to. Everything is in everything else. With the insight of interconnectedness or "interbeing," you understand that you *are* your father, you *are* your mother. If you are angry with your father or your mother, you are angry with yourself. Likewise, if you are angry with your children, you are angry with yourself. Our children are our continuation, and they carry us into the future.

The same is true with our loved one. Even if we are not related biologically, they are in us and it is impossible to take them out. All our shared experiences and everything they have ever thought, said, or done, lives on within us and cannot be undone or taken out of us. To reconnect with them, we only need to go inward and reconnect with ourselves.

This short guided meditation can help us visualize the reality of our loved ones within us. We can also substitute with the words "mother," "father," "grandmother," "grandfather," and "all my ancestors" in order to feel the connection to all our ancestors in us and to receive their energy and support.

Breathing in, I see the presence of my beloved in every cell of my body.
Breathing out, I smile to my beloved in every cell of my body.
My beloved in every cell,
Smiling.

Breathing in, my loved one is breathing in with me.
Breathing out, my loved one is breathing out with me.
My loved one breathing in with me
My loved one breathing out with me

Breathing in, I am breathing with my loved one's
lungs.
Breathing out, our bodies relax.
Breathing with my loved one's lungs,
Our bodies relaxing.

Breathing in, I am looking with my loved one's eyes.
Breathing out, I am listening with my loved one's ears.
Looking with my loved one's eyes
Listening with my loved one's ears

Breathing in, I see I am part of the wonderful river of
life, flowing continuously for thousands of years.
Breathing out, I smile and entrust myself to this
river of life.
River of life, entrusting myself.

HEALING THE PAST
IN THE PRESENT

The past is not truly gone; it is still here, and we can touch it. We may have regrets about the past and believe we cannot go back to fix our mistakes. In fact, touching the present moment, we can still touch the pain and the wounds of the past. We may think that those who have passed away are no longer here—our loved ones, family members, ancestors, or friends. But if we know how to touch the present moment deeply, we discover that they are all still there, alive within us, and we can still speak to them.

For example, looking deeply with the eyes of interbeing, I see that my mother is still alive within me. I am her continuation. I am my mother, and my mother is myself. It is possible to heal the wounds of the past right in the present moment. It is possible to apologize and express regret even if the person is no longer here.

"Mother, I am sorry, I was unskillful, and I know I hurt you. I will not say something like that again. Please forgive me." When my mother in me hears these words of reconciliation, she smiles, and my wounds begin to heal.

You can heal the wounds of the past by touching the present moment. This is the miracle of mindfulness.

LETTING EMOTIONS FLOW THROUGH YOU

Do not be afraid of your painful feelings and difficult emotions. If we try to repress our painful feelings, we create a lack of circulation in our psyche which can lead to depression or other psychological problems. Just as the body needs good circulation of the blood to remain healthy, we also need good psychological circulation. We need to allow our feelings and emotions to circulate. If suffering comes up, we embrace it with our mindfulness; we don't try to push it away.

Mindfulness is the blood of our psyche. Like the blood in the body, it has the power to eliminate toxins and heal our pain. Every time our pain is embraced by mindfulness, it loses some of its strength; it becomes weaker each time. In that way, we create good circulation in our psyche. When mindfulness circulates in our consciousness, we begin to experience well-being. We needn't be afraid of our pain when we know that our mindfulness is also there, ready to embrace and transform it.

THE WAY OUT
IS IN

To understand our suffering and our difficulties, we need to be there for ourselves. We need to come home and look inward. The first thing we should do is to recognize and admit that we are suffering. If we can acknowledge that we're suffering, we have a chance to transform that suffering. The second step is to have the courage to look deeply into our suffering, to listen to it, embrace it, and understand its nature. Many of us do everything we can to avoid going back to ourselves, because we're afraid that if we come home and touch the suffering inside, it will overwhelm us. That's why we need to train ourselves in the practice of mindfulness. Practicing mindful breathing, sitting, and walking allows us to generate an energy that can help us be stronger.

Looking deeply, we have a chance to understand our suffering and to see the way out. We go inward to take care of our painful feelings and emotions, to make transformation possible. The way out is in. When we understand our suffering, it transforms, and we feel renewed.

SELF-CARE
LISTENING TO A
MINDFULNESS BELL

One helpful way to reduce our stress, pain, and anxiety is to stop and breathe for at least three breaths every time we hear a "mindfulness bell." In a monastery or a practice center, bells are "invited to sound" many times a day, before, after, and sometimes during every activity. And in the world too, there are so many "bells" in our daily life—the telephone, a text message or notification, an alarm, a siren. These are all bells of mindfulness. The sound of the bell is our friend, reminding us to stop what we are doing and come home to ourselves and the present moment.

Whenever we hear a bell, we stop everything, both physically and mentally. We stop being carried away by our thinking and our worries, and we come back to focus on our breathing. We follow the breath as it goes in and out of the body for at least three full in- and out-breaths. This is so soothing. We bring our awareness back to our body and release any tension we are holding in the body. We do the same thing with our mind—we become aware of what we are thinking and how we are feeling. We practice mere recognition, making a note of our thoughts and feelings and then just letting them go. This practice is very easy and brings instant relief and calm. When we practice this throughout the day, it strengthens our "mindfulness muscle" and helps us remain calm even in difficult situations.

We can make good use of many different "bells"—meditation bells, church bells, a clock chiming, even a red light in traffic can be a bell of mindfulness, calling us back to our true home. Be creative—find your own bells of mindfulness and make a commitment to stop whenever you hear them. You might like to download a mindfulness bell onto your computer or phone and program it to sound at regular intervals. Then, each time you hear it, take a break from whatever you are doing. Stop. Breathe. Relax. Let go. This is a precious opportunity to reset the counter to zero. To touch a moment of peace and be fully alive. As you listen, you can say,

Listen, listen.
This wonderful sound
brings me back
to my true home.

CALL YOUR EMOTION BY ITS TRUE NAME

The mind is like a river and the mental formations—our feelings and emotions—are drops of water in succession, forming a stream. To meditate is to sit by the river of the mind and recognize every mental formation as it arises. We do not attempt to fight or to grasp onto anything. We just allow the mental formation to be there and recognize it, name it. This way it will calm down naturally.

With the practice of mindful breathing and walking, we can generate enough energy of mindfulness to allow us to come home to ourselves without fear. We do not risk being overwhelmed by our painful feelings and emotions. With the energy of mindfulness, we can recognize them, smile to them and say, "Hello my pain, my loneliness, my sorrow. I know you are there and I will take good care of you." "Hello my anger, my sadness, my fear. I am not running away from you anymore. I am determined to take good care of you."

We may like to write down a list of feelings and emotions so that we can recognize them easily and call them by their true names.

Knowing how to handle a painful feeling, a painful emotion, is key. It is possible to transform our feelings of anger or sorrow into understanding, acceptance, and compassion.

With the practice of mindfulness, we can learn how to generate a feeling of joy and happiness, gladdening the mind and creating a beautiful inner landscape. Here, too, it is helpful to name our feelings: "Hello my joy, my peace, my happiness. I know you are there, and I am so happy."

THE SECOND ARROW
OF SUFFERING

When an arrow strikes you, you feel intense pain, but if a second arrow strikes you in the same spot, the pain you feel is not double but ten times worse. Losing someone you love is the first arrow. You feel the acute pain of loss and sorrow. But worrying, being anxious, or succumbing to despair are like the second arrow.

When you are in pain, breathe in and out and recognize the pain, but don't exaggerate it. Don't allow the second arrow to strike. Our guilt, remorse, and regrets are the second arrows we often fire at ourselves.

SAYING SORRY TO A LOVED ONE WHO HAS PASSED

If we have said something unkind to someone who has passed away, such as our grandma, we can begin anew. We just sit down, practice mindful breathing in and out, and we ask our grandma to be there in us. We smile at her and sincerely say, "Grandma, I'm sorry. I will not say something like that again." And we'll see our grandma smiling. This practice will bring us peace; it will renew us and will bring a lot of joy and happiness to the people around us and to future generations.

SELF-CARE
BEGINNING ANEW WHEN A
LOVED ONE HAS DIED

Guilt, regret, and remorse can cause us unbearable suffering long after a loved one has died. Sometimes we carry these feelings with us for many years and suffer deeply each time we think of what we regret.

We may regret some things we said that were not very kind or loving, and we may also regret some things we didn't say to the person we love before they died. We may feel remorse for past actions that hurt them or regret that we neglected to do something important that we now wish we had. Often, we regret that we weren't kinder to our loved one during their lifetime or didn't show them enough how much we love them. Now we may feel it's too late. But we don't need to feel that kind of regret—our loved ones live on in us and we can speak to them whenever we want. We can apologize for our unskillfulness and ask for forgiveness. We can smile to them and say the things we should have said but didn't have the chance to say. Say it right now and they will hear it. We can begin anew with our loved one even after they have died.

THE GIFT OF
FORGIVENESS

When we lose someone we love, we often feel
burdened by guilt, especially if they died suddenly and we didn't have time to say goodbye.
If our loved one died in an accident, or if their
pain and suffering was so intolerable that they
took their own life, we may feel unbearable
grief and remorse.

*Could I have prevented this? Why wasn't I there for
them more? How can I forgive myself for the pain I've
caused? How can I apologize and ask for forgiveness
when my loved one is no longer here?* These are the
kinds of questions people often ask when they
have lost someone they love.

We may cry and scream, throw ourselves
on the floor or beat ourselves when the other
person dies because we remember that when
they were alive, there were times when we did

not treat them well. The complex of guilt causes us intense suffering.

It is so difficult to admit that we were so busy, that we weren't there for our loved one, that we didn't understand their suffering enough.

We need to know that everyone makes mistakes and is unskillful at times, but we can learn from our mistakes. The practice of mindfulness can transform the past and the insight of impermanence can help liberate us. With this insight, we do whatever we can today to make our loved ones happy. We don't wait for tomorrow, because tomorrow may be too late.

We also cultivate compassion for ourselves, forgive ourselves, and vow that from now on we will do better. If we know how to do better, we suffer less right away. We don't suffer the feeling of guilt anymore. We can begin to speak frankly and openly about death—the death of our father, the death of our son, of our partner, of our sibling. This is an opportunity for us to learn to live differently. We can no longer help our loved ones who have died, but there are so many people alive we can help today.

The fact is that we can liberate ourselves from the prison of the past. We can make a strong determination, a strong aspiration, to go out and help others, to help people in need, help the poor, the sick and elderly, the homeless people, those who have been abused. Helping others, we heal ourselves.

SELF-CARE
WRITE A LETTER TO BEGIN ANEW
WITH YOUR LOVED ONE

To help us relieve the guilt we may feel, we can write a letter of apology to the one who has died and ask for their forgiveness. We can call this kind of letter a love letter. Of course, we do not post this letter, but we can put it in a special place—perhaps on an altar we have created for them or next to a photo we have of them—and from time to time we can reread it to water the seeds of compassion and forgiveness within ourselves. Writing a love letter like this can be very transformative and healing. It can heal our loved one and ourselves.

Set aside plenty of time for yourself to write the letter. Before you begin writing, practice looking deeply into yourself and the nature of your relationship. Be honest with yourself. Why was communication difficult? Why was happiness not possible at times? Look deeply and ask yourself: What was my part in the difficulty between us? What was the other person's part? What were the conditions that led to the difficulty? Can you see that you were both doing the best you could with the conditions you had?

We can apologize if we feel regret or remorse for things we have said or done that we know must have hurt the other person deeply. "Please forgive me. What I said was very hurtful, and I know I caused you to suffer a lot. I deeply regret what I said, and I hope you can forgive me. I said such things because I was suffering, but now, I see the situation more clearly. I will do my best not to repeat the same mistakes in future." Expressing your remorse will help relieve the pain you are feeling.

REFLECTIONS BEFORE WRITING A LETTER

Before we write a love letter, we need to do some deep looking. Reflect deeply and honestly on the following points and make notes before writing your letter.

Recognize your shortcomings, failings, and all the things you wish you had done differently in your relationship with your loved one.

Also recognize your positive qualities, what you did do that was good—good intentions, kind, loving, or generous thoughts, words, or actions. Make a list. Strive for balance—a roughly equal list of things you are happy about and not so happy about.

Look into all the causes and conditions that helped shape who you are—your childhood, your parents, your family situation, the schools you went to, and the society and culture in which you grew up.

Learn to accept that you did the best you could, given the conditions you had. Learn to accept your imperfections. Forgive yourself—when there is understanding and insight, forgiveness arises naturally.

Look deeply into the other person in the same way to see their strengths, weaknesses, and challenges and to gain more understanding and insight.

Water their flowers—express your gratitude and appreciation for them. Be concrete and mention specific examples of the things you are grateful to them for and the qualities in them you admire.

Express your regrets and apologize for your shortcomings and mistakes. Again, be specific.

Ask for forgiveness and promise you will try to do better in the future.

If we are able to write such a letter, we will feel great relief. The love, understanding, and compassion we feel for ourselves will grow as well as the love, understanding, and compassion for the other person. Like this, we feel a deeper, more compassionate and lasting connection with our loved one.

Our loved ones do not want us to suffer after they die—they want us to be happy. We may hold on to grief, believing that our deep grief and despair is a measure of the depth of our love for the person we have lost. Or we may continue to torture ourselves with feelings of guilt, remorse, and regret.

But the real question is not whether our loved ones can forgive us for our failings, but if we can forgive ourselves. Do we have enough compassion for ourselves? Can we see that we were doing the best we could with the conditions we had at the time?

To help us cultivate self-compassion, we need to look deeply into ourselves and into the relationship with our loved one. Everything is co-created. The situation came to be because of an infinite number of causes and conditions. When we can see that *this* is because *that* is, we feel lighter. When we understand that we were doing the best we could, and that we are always doing the best we can with what we have, we feel less burdened. We can accept our shortcomings and forgive ourselves.

Getting in touch with our inner child can help us understand ourselves better, accept our shortcomings, and cultivate compassion for ourselves. The small, wounded child within us suffers greatly when we lose someone we love. This loss touches on our earlier losses and unhealed wounds, compounding the pain we feel. The practice of guided meditation can be very helpful to establish connection with our inner child and deepen our understanding and compassion.

Children are so easily hurt. An overly severe glance or a threatening or reproachful word from a parent can wound deeply and cause us to feel shame. At five years old, we were very vulnerable, fragile, and impressionable. The wounds we received at that time and the beliefs we formed still lie deep within us. So, we have to be very gentle, loving, and understanding with our inner five-year-old child.

In this meditation, we go home and connect with the five-year-old child in us, the child that may still be deeply wounded, and that we have neglected for a long time. When we see ourselves as a five-year-old, compassion is born in our heart.

To help us cultivate compassion for ourselves and deepen our insight, we need to get in touch with our inner child and listen to them, not ignore or abandon them. Understanding the wounds and pain of our inner child gives rise to compassion and love. Love is understanding. When we are able to touch and recognize our inner pain, we have a chance to take care of it and transform it. Meditating on who we were as a child brings insight into our current suffering.

Breathing in and out with mindfulness, you can say,

Breathing in, I see myself as a five-year-old child
Breathing out, I smile with compassion to the five-year-old child in me

Breathing in, I see how innocent, vulnerable, and fragile I was at the age of five
Breathing out, I embrace and comfort my wounded inner child

Breathing in, I see my inner child is still very much alive within me
Breathing out, I listen deeply to the child in me.

When we understand the suffering of our parents, we can accept their shortcomings more easily. This helps us to understand the root of our own suffering and helps us accept our own shortcomings more easily, too. If you wish, you can continue the meditation thinking about your parents or guardians as small children. Like you, they were also young, vulnerable, and easily wounded. Like you, they may still carry wounds and suffering within them.

"Breathing in, I see my mother/father/guardian as a five-year-old child / Breathing out, I smile to them with compassion," and so on.

When we are in touch with the suffering our parents experienced as children, compassion is born in our hearts. This compassion has the capacity to heal us and our relationships. With compassion and understanding, forgiveness can arise.

I WALK FOR YOU

Many of my ancestors and many friends from my generation have already passed away. A good friend of mine is in a wheelchair and can't walk. Another friend has such pain in his knees that he can't walk up and down stairs. So, I walk for them. When I breathe in, I say to myself, "It's wonderful that I am still able to walk like this." With that awareness, I can enjoy every step. I say, "Breathing in, I know I am alive! Breathing out, I smile to life." Mindfulness reminds me to notice and enjoy that my body is alive and strong enough for me to walk.

Sometimes I say that I walk for my mother or that my father is enjoying walking with me. I walk for my father. I walk for my mother. I walk for my teacher. I walk for my students. Your father may not have known how to walk mindfully and enjoy every moment, so you can walk for him. This way you both benefit and experience healing.

SUFFERING IS
NOT ENOUGH

Life is filled with suffering, but it is also filled with many wonders, such as the blue sky, the sunshine, the eyes of a baby. Life is not only suffering. We can learn to be in touch with the wonders of life. They are within us and all around us, everywhere, anytime.

A CLOUD

NEVER DIES

A FREE WHITE CLOUD

Now you are free.
The chains can no longer confine your true body.
You return to your life as a white cloud
just like before—
a white cloud
utterly free
in the immense sky.

LOOK DEEPLY TO SEE YOUR BELOVED IN OTHER FORMS

On a beautiful sunny day, you may look up into the sky and see a nice, puffy cloud floating by. You admire its shape, the way the light falls upon its many folds and the shadow it casts on the green field. You fall in love with this cloud. You want it to stay with you and keep you happy. But then its shape and color start to change. The sky becomes dark, and it begins to rain. The cloud is no longer apparent to you. It has become rain. You begin to cry for the return of your beloved cloud.

But when the cloud transforms itself into rain, you can look deeply into the rain and see that your cloud is still there, laughing and smiling at you.

NOTHING DIES, EVERYTHING TRANSFORMS

Before the cloud appeared in the sky, it existed in another form—as mist, ocean, rain, or river. If we look deeply into the nature of a cloud, we see that a cloud can't die; it can't pass from a state of being into a state of nonbeing. A cloud can become rain or snow or ice, but it can't become nothing. So if the sky is clear, it doesn't mean that your cloud has died. It continues on in other forms.

How can our loved one die? Everything arises in dependence on everything else. There's no beginning or ending; there's no creation and no destruction of anything at all. This is true of the entire universe. Billions and billions of conditions have come together for us to manifest in this form. When different conditions arise, we will manifest in a different form.

Do not get caught in the form. Do not get caught in signs. Learn to look with "the eyes of signlessness" and see your cloud in its new forms—in the rain, in the river, in your tea.

If you have lost someone and if you have cried so very much, please look deeply and recognize that the true nature of your beloved is the nature of no birth and no death, no coming and no going.

ALLOWING
OURSELVES TO
FEEL HAPPY

We don't have to wait for the end of all our suffering before we can feel happy again. We are allowed to feel happy *now*. But we may need to change our idea of happiness to recognize the happiness that is available to us right here and right now. Our idea of happiness may itself be the obstacle keeping us from true happiness.

Lotus flowers need mud to grow; they cannot grow on marble. Without suffering, happiness is not possible. So, if you know *how* to suffer, you don't suffer as much anymore, and out of our suffering, a lotus flower of happiness can grow.

We can use our suffering to generate happiness, understanding, and love. When we embrace our suffering and look deeply into it, we can understand it better, and we can better understand the suffering of others, too. With this comes compassion and forgiveness.

Understanding and love are the foundation of happiness. By embracing our suffering, understanding it, and tending to it, love and compassion will be generated.

So, we see that happiness and suffering are two sides of the same coin. They inter-are. We cannot have one without the other.

RESTORATIVE DEEP RELAXATION

When we fall down, we have physical pain. When we're sad or anxious, we call it emotional pain. But mind and body are not separate, and suffering is not just an emotion. When we suffer a deep loss, especially if it was sudden and traumatic, the shock can lodge in our body. We hold our suffering in every muscle and in every cell. The practice of deep relaxation is a way to acknowledge and soothe the suffering in both the body and mind. We take time to be there for ourselves, to offer ourselves tenderness, love, and care.

Deep relaxation begins with observing the breath in the body. You can do this sitting up or lying down, but lying on the ground allows us to feel the different parts of the body more easily as we surrender ourselves to the gentle force of gravity and to the earth beneath us. At a time when we may be feeling vulnerable, wounded, or numbed with shock, lying on the ground helps us connect with the earth's strength and solidity and her calming and healing energy.

HOW TO RELAX DEEPLY

Lie comfortably on your back, with your legs and arms outstretched. Become aware of the air moving in and out of your body. Feel your abdomen gently rising and falling. With each out-breath, allow yourself to relax a little more and let go of the tension you are holding. Become aware of all the points of contact between your body and the ground.

Now bring your awareness to your head. Feel the weight of your head and imagine it is sinking into the ground. Breathe out and relax. Bring your awareness to your eyes. "Breathing in, I'm aware of my eyes. Breathing out, I smile to my eyes with gratitude and love." Feel the healing energy of gratitude arise in you that—no matter how poor your eyesight is—your eyes allow you to experience a multitude of colors and forms: the blue sky, the setting sun, the green trees, and the faces of those you love.

Then bring your awareness down to your nose, your mouth, your throat, your shoulders, your back, and continue on down to your toes. You're doing a scan of your body, not with an x-ray, but with a ray of mindfulness. You go through your whole body, bringing your awareness to each part and to each organ, relaxing it and sending it healing and loving energy. "Breathing in, I'm aware of my heart. Breathing out, I smile to my heart with love and compassion. I send my heart loving and healing energy and feel grateful I have a heart. My heart beats day and night for me, keeping me alive. Even if my heart is aching or does not work as well as it once did, I'm so grateful to have a heart. I apologize for the many ways I have mistreated you in the past, and for the many times I haven't listened to you. I often forget I have a heart at all and take you for granted. But now I promise to take good care of you. Thank you for being there for me."

Continue through all the parts of your body in a similar way. Smile to every cell and let go of tension. Let your love and gratitude soothe and heal you. Afterwards you will feel restored and at peace. Try to keep the soft and calming energy of mindfulness alive in you for as long as possible when you get up again. Make this a daily practice and experience gentle healing and transformation.

TOUCHING THE
ULTIMATE

Once, as I was about to step on a dry leaf, I saw the leaf in the ultimate dimension of reality. I saw that it was not really dead, but it was merging with the moist soil and preparing to appear on the tree the following spring. I smiled at the leaf and said, "You are pretending."

Everything is pretending to be born and pretending to die. When conditions are sufficient, the body reveals itself, and we say the body exists. When conditions are not sufficient, the body cannot be perceived by us, and we say the body no longer exists. However, the day of our so-called death is a day of our continuation in many other forms. If you know how to touch your loved one in the ultimate dimension, they will always be there with you and inside you. This is a deep practice and can relieve our suffering when we lose someone.

YOU AND YOUR BELOVED ARE NEVER SEPARATE

When we look deeply into a flower, we can see that it's made of many different elements. In fact, it is made exclusively of non-flower elements. The entire universe can be seen in a flower. We can see the sunshine that helped it grow, the rain, the soil, the seed, and even the gardener. If we took away any one of these elements, there would be no flower left. The flower does not exist on its own; it is inextricably interconnected with everything else.

Like the flower, we, too, are made only of non-self elements. We are made of the rain, the sun, the earth, our parents, our society. If you remove any of these non-self elements, we would not exist. And like the flower, we are interconnected with all other beings and with the entire cosmos. You cannot be by yourself alone. You have to inter-be with all else. Nothing exists on its own, all things inter-are.

YOUR LOVED ONE
WILL ALWAYS BE
WITH YOU

If you establish yourself in the present moment, and touch the present moment deeply, you can gain deep insight into who you are. If I am really in touch with myself, I discover that at the same time I am the sun, I am a cloud, I am the earth, a river, a mountain, a squirrel, a tree. Everything is in everything else. Could I even be here without the squirrel, without the mountain, without the cloud? If you took the mountain out of me, I would no longer be here. If you took the cloud out of me, I would not be here either because actually I *am* all these things.

I am the cloud, the squirrel, the deer, the mountain. I am my loved one. You cannot take my loved one out of me. This is the insight of *interbeing* that I can touch when I touch the present moment deeply. When you touch the one, you touch the all.

If you can see yourself as a leaf, as a flower, as a beautiful cloud in the sky, you will easily understand that you have never been born, you have not come from nowhere, and you will never die. And you can never be without the ones you love.

When it rains,
we think there's no sunshine.
But above the clouds,
the sun shines brightly in the blue sky.

RELATIVE AND ULTIMATE DIMENSIONS OF REALITY

In what we call the historical dimension, we have birth certificates and death certificates. The day someone you love passes away, you suffer. If someone sits close to you and shows their concern, you feel some relief.

You have their friendship, their support, their warm hand to hold. This is the world of waves. It is characterized by birth and death, ups and downs, being and nonbeing.

A wave has a beginning and an end, but we cannot ascribe these characteristics to water. In the world of water, there is no birth or death, no being or nonbeing, no beginning or end. When we touch the water, we touch reality in its ultimate dimension and are liberated from all of these concepts.

THE DEEPEST
KIND OF RELIEF

Meditation is to live each moment of life deeply. Through meditation, we see that waves are made of water, and that the historical and the ultimate dimensions of reality are one. Even while living in the world of waves, we touch the water, knowing that a wave is nothing but water. We suffer if we touch only the waves. But if we learn how to stay in touch with the water, we feel a great relief.

We come to the practice seeking relief in the historical dimension. We calm our body and mind, and establish our stillness, our freshness, and our solidity. We practice loving-kindness, concentration, and transforming our anger, and we feel some relief.

But when we touch the ultimate dimension of reality, we get the deepest kind of relief. Each of us has the capacity to touch nirvana and be free from ideas of birth and death, one and many, coming and going.

SELF-CARE
TOUCHING THE EARTH

Many spiritual traditions have a practice of prostrating or touching the earth—to express respect and humility, to seek solace, and to reconnect with ourselves and with the earth. Touching the earth may be considered by some a devotional practice, but this is not necessarily so. To touch the earth is an act of deep surrender. We have come from the earth and we will go back to the earth, so, when we prostrate or lie down and touch the earth, we surrender everything to her.

We surrender ourselves and release all our suffering and sorrow and, above all, we release the notion that we are a separate self. The earth accepts and transforms whatever she receives, without discrimination. In return, we benefit from the earth's wholesome and healing energy, allowing the balm of her compassion to penetrate our heart. We receive the earth's solidity, her powerfully regenerative, creative, and healing energy.

We have all witnessed how the earth can take refuse, garbage, or compost, and transform it into beautiful flowers. We know that we, too, have this capacity. The earth embraces us and helps us transform our suffering and despair.

HOW TO TOUCH THE EARTH

Wherever we are, whether in a meditation hall, at home in a quiet place, in front of our shrine or altar, or in a peaceful place outside in nature, we can lie down on the earth to receive her qualities of strength, stability, and forbearance. We can be in a prostrate position, on our knees with our forehead on the floor—similar to the child's pose in yoga, with our arms outstretched in front of us. If you prefer, you can lie face down on the earth, outstretched. As we touch the earth, we gently follow our breathing and connect to our body, to our animal, plant, and mineral ancestors and to the earth beneath us. We release all our sadness, fear, and worry. We release all the tension in our body and mind. We maintain an open and receptive attitude. We know the earth can absorb our suffering and negativity without reacting or judging us. In this way, we're able to transform those things within us which are painful and difficult. With this practice, we cultivate a relationship with ourselves and the earth and, in doing so, we restore our balance, our wholeness, and our peace.

Touch the earth in silence and stay in that position for at least three long in- and out-breaths. The longer you remain in contact with the earth, the easier it is to let go of any tension, pain, or suffering and to relax into a state of complete surrender and peace.

TOUCHING THE EARTH,
CALLING ON OUR ANCESTORS

In times of great suffering, we can also call on the stream of all our land, spiritual, and blood ancestors in us to lend us their support.

As you lie on the ground, your palms facing upward in a position of surrender, imagine one hand represents your mother and the other represents your father. This is not just imagination—your hands really *are* your father's hands, your mother's hands, your grandfather's hands and so on. If you look deeply, you can see this clearly. Your hands are not yours alone. They have come down to you from all your ancestors.

Now bring to mind all the positive qualities of your mother and father—their wisdom, their strength, their skills and talents, their compassion—and feel those qualities within yourself. Consider all their weaknesses and shortcomings—which are also yours—and release these to the earth to be transformed. Allow yourself to be strengthened, nourished, and comforted by the positive qualities of your parents and ancestors, and release your suffering and theirs into the earth.

When you sit up, look deeply into your two hands to see your parents' hands or your grandparents' hands. Then bring your palms together to unite the qualities of your parents in you, hold your face in their hands or cross your arms over your heart to give yourself a hug. Feel your mother and father, your grandmother and grandfather, and all of your ancestors embracing and supporting you. Allow yourself to be held and comforted by them.

ASHES TO ASHES

When we say that humans go from ashes to
ashes and from dust to dust, it doesn't sound
very joyful or comforting because none of us
wants to come from or return to dust. But it
is our mind of discrimination that thinks this
way, because we don't know what dust really is.
For scientists, a speck of dust is incredibly excit-
ing. Every atom is a vast mystery. We still have
not yet fully understood atoms, electrons, and
nuclei. A particle of dust is a marvel.

WE ARE LIFE

We are in the habit of identifying ourselves
with our bodies. The idea that we are this body
is deeply entrenched in us. But your loved
one is not just their body; they are much more
than that. According to the twentieth-century
French philosopher Jean-Paul Sartre: *"L'homme
est la somme de ses actes."* We are the sum of our
actions. This is what karma means: action. Our
thoughts, speech and physical actions are our
karma. We are the sum of our three actions,
and not only do these three actions continue us
into the future but they have an effect on others
and the world in every moment, even while we
are alive. They are our true legacy.

The idea that "This body is me and I am this
body" is a belief we must let go of. If we do not,
we will suffer a great deal. We are *life,* and life is
far vaster than this body, this concept, this mind.

WE ARE NOT LIMITED TO OUR LIFESPAN

Most of us believe we will spend seventy, eighty, ninety, or one hundred years on this planet and then we'll be gone. But when we look deeply, we see this is a wrong perception.

Your lifespan is not limited to seventy, eighty, or one hundred years, and that is good news. Your body is not your self; you are much more than this body. You are life without boundaries.

We are not limited to our physical body, even when we are alive. We *inter-are* with our ancestors, our descendants, and the whole of the cosmos. We do not have a separate self; we are interconnected with all of life, and we, and everything, are always in transformation.

DEATH MAKES LIFE POSSIBLE

Life is made of death, and death is made of life. We have to accept death; it makes life possible. The cells in our body are dying every day, but we never think to organize funerals for them. The death of one cell allows for the birth of another. Life and death are two aspects of the same reality. This deep meditation brings forth non-fear, non-anger, and non-despair.

A CLOUD CAN NEVER DIE

In our mind, to die means from something you become nothing; from someone you become no one. If we look deeply, we see that reality is not like this. The cloud does not come from nothing. It has come from the water in the rivers, the lakes, the ocean, and the heat of the sunshine. Equally, we believe that to be born means from nothing we become something. From no-one we suddenly become someone. You did not come from nowhere before you were born, and you cannot become nothing when you die. Like the cloud, your nature and the nature of your loved one is also the nature of no birth and no death.

You can be with death peacefully if you know how to touch your true nature of no-birth and no-death. A drop of rain falling on the ground disappears in no time at all. And yet somehow it is still there even if it is absorbed into the soil and no longer visible. If it evaporates, it is still there in the air—it has become vapor. You no longer see the drop of water but that doesn't mean it's not there. A cloud can become rain or snow or ice, but a cloud cannot become nothing. A cloud can never die.

OUR TRUE NATURE

Those of us who have lost a loved one know what grief is. But if you know how to look with eyes of signlessness—if you are not trapped in the form of your loved one—you can overcome your grief and sorrow. You are capable of going beyond form and signs to understand that nothing is born, and nothing dies. There is only transformation. Everything continues in a new form. You, too, are the same. Your nature is the nature of deathlessness.

As soon as the notion of birth and death dies, real life is born.

PASSED AWAY DOES NOT MEAN GONE

The eighteenth-century French scientist Antoine Lavoisier famously declared: *"Rien ne se crée, rien ne se perd; tout se transforme."* Nothing is created, nothing is destroyed. Everything transforms. Matter can become energy and energy can be transformed into matter, but we cannot create or destroy either one. Similarly, our beloved has simply taken on another form. We can see our loved one in everything—in a cloud, in a child, in the breeze.

Smiling, we can say, "Dear one, I know you are there very close to me. I know that your nature is the nature of no birth and no death. I know that I have not lost you; you are always with me."

If you look deeply, you will see your loved one in every moment of your daily life. Their true nature is the nature of not born and not dying, not arriving and not departing.

OUR THOUGHTS, SPEECH, AND ACTIONS LIVE ON

The thoughts and feelings we send out into the world have a powerful effect. Every thought we produce, everything we think, say, and do, is an action. These actions continue forever. They cannot disappear, but, just like the cloud, they can transform.

So when this body disintegrates, it's not the end. This body is only a very small part of you. What you produce every day in terms of thought, speech, and action is already out there and cannot be taken back, cannot be undone. You may not be able to see it, just as you don't see the water vapor that will eventually form a cloud, but it is there. So, when you look at your body, you have to remember that this is only a very small part of you. The greater part of you is already out there.

We don't need to wait for the complete disintegration of this body to begin to see ourselves in others, just as a cloud doesn't need to have been entirely transformed into rain in order to see that part of herself is already down on Earth in the form of a river, part of herself is still falling as rain, and part of herself is still a cloud in the sky. The cloud smiles down to herself as the rain and the river and says "Enjoy your journey! I will join you very soon."

The fruits of our thoughts, speech, and actions are what continue us when this body disintegrates. They bear our signature. When our loved one's body disintegrates, this is what will continue them. Everything they have ever said, thought, or done has had an impact on others and the world. This is what continues in many different manifestations. All your loved one's deepest aspirations, their beliefs, their thoughts, words, and deeds, will manifest in countless new and wonderful forms. That is where you can find them.

SELF-CARE
SEEING YOUR LOVED ONE ALIVE
IN YOU AND ALL AROUND YOU

Bring to mind all the people your loved one knew and came into contact with during their lifetime—their friends, their family (children, parents, siblings), people they worked with, people they went to school with, and write a list or draw a web diagram of their many relationships. Look deeply to see how your loved one is still alive in all these people, as well as in yourself.

If you can, speak to some of these people. Ask them to share stories. What do they remember most, and what do they treasure about your loved one? This is nourishing and healing for both you and the other person. Whenever you miss your loved one, speak to one of the people who knew them well.

What ideas have you inherited from your loved one? You might bring to mind the work they did and projects they accomplished, their good deeds. Recall all the ways they have changed the world, no matter how big or small. It is often the small things that touch us most deeply.

o o o

Sometimes we know exactly how our loved one would feel about something—whether they would like this food or drink, this book or film, this scenery, this person or activity. Keep an open dialogue going with your loved one. You can ask them if they like the taste of the food you are eating. Would they like to go here or there with you? This is a way to keep the connection alive with your loved one. You can also ask them their opinion about important decisions, and you may be surprised to find they will give you good advice.

What are the most memorable things your loved one ever said to you? What are some of the kindest, most generous, most courageous, most adventurous things your loved one ever did?

∘ ∘ ∘

Sometimes we cannot transform our grief because we believe our loved one suffered terribly during their lifetime. This may be true, but it is not the *whole* truth. There were times when your loved one didn't suffer, when they were happy and healthy and enjoying life. We need to have a more balanced view. Try to recall the happy moments, the joyful moments, all the times you saw your loved one laugh and be happy. The more you reflect on this, the more happy moments will come to mind. This can bring us great relief.

TOUCHING THE WONDERS OF LIFE

When you have a moment alone, you might like to use that time to come home to yourself and touch the wonders of life. Instead of allowing yourself to be caught up in the past or the future, or carried away by distractions or strong emotions in the present, pay attention to your breath and come home to the present moment.

We breathe in and out all day, but we are not aware that we are breathing in and breathing out. "Breathing in, I know I am alive. Breathing out, I smile to life." This is a very simple practice. If we go home to our in-breath and out-breath and breathe mindfully, we become fully alive in the here and now.

In our daily lives, our bodies are present, but our minds might be elsewhere, caught in our worries, and our anxieties. Life is only available in the present moment. The past is already gone; the future is not yet here. When we establish ourselves in the present moment, we are able to live our life deeply and get in touch with the healing, refreshing, and nourishing elements that are always within us and around us.

Every second of life is filled with precious jewels. Those jewels are our awareness of our breath, our body, our feelings, the earth the sky, the trees, the river, the ocean, the birds, and other animals—all the miracles inside us and around us.

GRATITUDE
FOR LIFE

The seed of suffering in you may be strong right now, but don't wait until you have no more suffering before allowing yourself to be happy.

You don't have to wait ten years to experience happiness. It is present in every moment of your daily life; we just need to recognize the conditions for happiness that are available right now.

There are those of us who are alive but don't appreciate being alive. When you breathe in, and you are aware of your in-breath, you touch the miracle of being alive. Being alive is a true source of joy and happiness.

The conditions for our happiness are already sufficient. We only need to allow ourselves to be fully alive in the present moment, and we will be able to touch them. Mindfulness is the lamp we light up that lets us recognize that we have many conditions for happiness even in the midst of suffering.

SUNFLOWERS
IN APRIL

In summer, the hills around Plum Village are covered with hundreds of thousands of sunflowers. But if you come in the month of April, the hills are bare. Yet when the farmers walk through their fields, they can already see the sunflowers. They know that the soil has been prepared, the seeds have been planted, the rains are good, that every condition is sufficient but one. The one condition that's missing is time. With time, the heat of the summer months will allow the sunflowers to grow tall and blossom. Sunflowers depend on many conditions in order to manifest, not just one, and all are equally important. In the sunflowers we see the earth, the minerals, the farmer, and we see time and space. When all the necessary conditions come together, the sunflowers will manifest. When the conditions are not sufficient, the sunflowers will hide.

Who can say that your loved one has passed away? When you touch your loved one in the ultimate dimension, you see that they are still with you. The same is true of a flower. A flower may pretend to be born, but it has always been there in other forms, in the soil, the rain, the sunshine. Later the flower may pretend to die, but it is just playing a game of hide-and-seek. The flower reveals itself to us and then hides itself again. If we are attentive, we can see it anytime we want.

We need to recognize the interbeing nature of all that is. In the light of interbeing, life and death are not separate. They inter-are. We cannot have one without the other, like happiness and suffering, darkness and light. They lean on each other. They contain each other.

WE LIVE FOR THOSE
WHO HAVE DIED

When a natural disaster occurs, in times of war
and genocide, when atrocities are committed
and hundreds of thousands of people die, people
everywhere suffer, including people on the
other side of the world. All of us suffer when so
many people die, not just those who are directly
involved. We may ask ourselves how God could
allow such terrible things to happen. Why do
babies, children, and so many people have to
die? Why them and not us? We ask so many
questions but do not have the answers. We just
suffer.

I also suffer with you. But I practice. I sit
down and practice looking deeply. I see that
when others die, we too die, because we are
deeply interconnected. When the one you love
dies, somehow you die with them. Seeing that
they are no longer able to live, we have to live

for them. We have to live in such a way that a future is possible for our children and their children. The way we choose to live our life after they have gone can give their death meaning. This is the insight of interbeing—everything is in everything else. They are us and we are them. When they die, a part of us dies, too. When we continue to live, they continue to live with us.

With this insight, we do not suffer any more. We know how to continue them in us, how to carry them into the future with us, and how to create a bright future for them. With this insight, we experience peace.

WE SEND LIGHT OUT ALL AROUND US

We are like candles. We send light out all around us, radiating in all directions. All our thoughts, words, and actions are our light. If we say something kind, our kind words will go out in many directions, and we go along with them. Your loved one's kind thoughts and kind deeds also travel in many directions, never ending. We are transforming and being continued in different forms every moment.

Our thoughts, words, and deeds are our legacy. They live on long after we are no longer there.

NOTHING
IS LOST

Have you ever played with a kaleidoscope? When you look into a kaleidoscope, you see a beautiful image of many colors. Just a small movement is enough to make something miraculous appear. A tableau of colors and forms reveals itself, an amazing manifestation. You marvel at this breathtaking image for a second or two, then you turn the kaleidoscope and another equally stunning manifestation appears. Should we cry every time one of these manifestations comes to an end? There is no need to feel regret when we lose one of these beautiful images, because now there is a new image to delight in.

In our current form, we are a beautiful manifestation that Mother Earth has helped to create. When this manifestation is over, we will manifest in another way. Being a cloud may be wonderful, but being rain falling to the Earth is also wonderful.

Things manifest, then disappear, and manifest again in another form—thousands upon thousands of times. If you look deeply, you will see this reality. We manifest, then disappear. Nothing is lost. Nothing is born, and nothing dies. It's a game of hide-and-seek. There is no creation, only manifestation. There is no death, only transformation.

YOU CANNOT
KILL ANYONE

Martin Luther King Jr., Gandhi, John F. Kennedy, even Jesus Christ, were all killed by people who suffered enormously, by people who believed they could kill these great leaders and everything they represented. But what they didn't realize is that you cannot kill anyone. You cannot kill Martin Luther King or Jesus or Gandhi. After their deaths, they became bigger, stronger, and more alive than before.

You cannot die, and you cannot kill anyone. Martin Luther King Jr., Jesus Christ, and Gandhi are all still very much alive in every one of us.

THE WATER AND
THE WAVE

We should be able to touch both dimensions of life: the historical and the ultimate. The wave exists in the historical dimension where there is birth and death, up and own, inside and outside, whereas the water belongs to the ultimate dimension, or nirvana. In the ultimate dimension there is no more birth or death, beginning or ending. We are usually just in touch with the wave, but when we discover how to touch the water, we receive the highest fruit that meditation can offer.

When the wave looks back on itself and realizes that it is both the wave and the water, it is no longer afraid of dying. It sees how the wave is born, how it swells, breaks, and dies, but it also sees that the contents of the wave are to be found in all the other waves. The ground of its being, and the ground of all the waves, is water. With this insight, it touches the ultimate dimension and is free of all fear of birth and death.

Practice like a wave. Take the time to look deeply into yourself and recognize that your true nature is the nature of no-birth and no-death. With this understanding, you can break through to freedom and fearlessness. If you carry deep grief within yourself, if you have lost a loved one, if you are inhabited by the fear of death, oblivion, or annihilation, please take up this teaching and begin to practice it, reminding yourself that while you are living the life of a wave, you are also the water. Touching the water, understanding the deepest truth of no birth and no death, we can touch peace.

TOUCHING NIRVANA

The wave can live her life as a wave, and at the same time she can live the life of water. She does not have to die in order to become water, because the wave is water already in the present moment.

Nirvana means the extinction of all notions and concepts, including the concepts of birth and death, being and nonbeing, coming and going, but it does not mean the extinction of life. Nirvana is the ultimate dimension of life, a state of coolness, peace, and joy. It is not a state to be attained after you die. You can touch nirvana right now by breathing, walking, and drinking your tea in mindfulness. Everything and everyone are dwelling in nirvana. You have been "nirvanized" since the very non-beginning of time!

If we can live our daily life deeply, we'll be able to touch nirvana right in the here and the now.

No coming, no going.
No after, no before.
I hold you close to me.
I release you to be so free,
because I am in you
and you are in me.

CONNECTING

WITH LIFE

Earth brings us to life
and nourishes us.
Earth takes us back again.

NATURE IS ALWAYS THERE FOR US

We can learn a lot from the earth's healing qualities. The earth is steadfast. She embodies perseverance, equanimity, and forbearance in the face of challenge. We, too, have these qualities. The earth is right here, inside us, and all around us. She supports us in very concrete and tangible ways. She gives birth to us and sustains us with her precious gifts of air, water, earth, and fire.

When we suffer, the Earth embraces us, helping us restore our energy and regain our strength. When we understand our deep connection to the Earth, we will have enough love and strength to continue.

When we suffer, we need love and understanding, yet we often hope that someone else will give us all the love, compassion, and understanding that we long for. We don't realize we can cultivate this for ourselves. Nature can help us cultivate this love and compassion. Nature is generous and abundant—she is always there for us. She provides everything we need.

THE DANDELION IS
SMILING FOR YOU

At the end of a retreat in California, a friend wrote this poem:

I have lost my smile, but don't worry.
The dandelion has it.

If you have lost your smile and yet are still capable of seeing that a dandelion is keeping it for you, there is hope. You still have enough mindfulness to see that your smile is there somewhere. The dandelion is a member of your community of friends. It is there, quietly and faithfully keeping your smile for you until you can smile again.

In fact, everything around you is keeping your smile for you. You don't need to feel lonely or isolated. You only need to open yourself to the support that is all around you, and inside you.

SEEING THE GOOD IN OUR LOVED ONE

When we practice the art of mindful living, we water the positive elements in ourselves and each other. We see that our beloved, like us, has both flowers and garbage inside, and we accept this. Our practice is to water the flower in our loved one, and not bring them more garbage.

When we try to grow flowers, if they don't grow well, we don't blame them or argue with them. The memory of our loved one is a flower. If we take care of her well, she will grow beautifully. If we take care of her poorly, she will wither. To help a flower grow well, we must understand her nature.

SELF-CARE
MAKING AN ALTAR FOR
YOUR LOVED ONE

When we have lost someone we love, we often feel the need to express our deep love and gratitude to them. We want to offer them something. And we want to keep their memory alive.

Making a shrine or altar for our loved one at home is a concrete way of expressing our love and care, and of helping us feel connected to them. We can set up a small table and place a photograph of our loved one, a candle, some flowers, and other meaningful things on it. We may like to include items representing our spiritual tradition if we have one, or things collected in nature—perhaps a stone, a leaf, a shell, or a flower. You may also like to place something on the altar that had special meaning for your loved one.

To help us feel connected and maintain communication, we can write to our loved one—a note, a love letter, an appreciation, or an apology—and put it on the altar. Some people like to light a candle, or offer incense, flowers, or their loved one's favorite food. On special days, such as ceremonial days during the initial period of mourning, on your loved one's birthday, or the anniversary of their death, we can prepare our loved one's favorite dishes or treats and place them on the altar. After the ceremony, everyone can enjoy eating them together, creating a feeling of intimacy and joy.

○ ○ ○

Placing objects on an altar doesn't mean we're worshiping these things. Creating and maintaining a home altar is a way to pay respect and express our love and gratitude to our loved one, our ancestors, and the world around us. It helps us remember that whatever we love, respect, and care deeply about is also within us.

Keep the altar fresh and beautiful, cleaning it and tending to it every day with mindfulness, love, and concentration. This helps us maintain our connection to our loved one. We can speak to them and tell them everything that is going on for us. We can announce all the news to our loved one, and to all our ancestors at the same time. We may like to tell our loved one that whatever they may not have finished or healed in their lifetime, we are doing our best to accomplish for them. This is the way to establish deep ongoing connections with our loved one and with the stream of life of which we are a part.

YOU WILL NOT SUFFER FOREVER

We see that all mental formations such as compassion, joy, love, fear, sorrow, and despair are organic in nature. When any of these seeds are watered in us, they manifest in our mind consciousness as mental formations. We don't need to be afraid of a difficult or uncomfortable emotion because by embracing it with mindfulness, transformation is always possible. When a feeling of sadness comes up, we breathe and say to ourselves:

> *Breathing in, I know there is a feeling of sadness in me*
> *Breathing out, I embrace this feeling of sadness and let it calm down.*

We know that everything is impermanent, including our feelings and emotions. They come, they stay for a while, and then they go again. We just notice and name the difficult emotions as they arise, and they will calm down and begin to transform on their own. This is the power of mere recognition. We simply recognize our thoughts and feelings as they arise.

By having this deep insight into the organic nature of mental formations, we become a lot calmer, more stable and peaceful. We know that this too will pass. Our pain will eventually subside. With just a smile and mindful breathing, we begin to transform our suffering.

WE DON'T
WALK ALONE

When we walk, we're not walking alone. Our parents and ancestors are always walking with us. They're present in every cell of our body. So each step that brings us peace, healing, and happiness also brings peace, healing, and happiness to our parents and ancestors. We have the power to transform the past. Every mindful step has the power to transform us and all our ancestors within us, including spiritual ancestors and our animal, plant, and mineral ancestors. We don't walk for ourselves alone. When we walk, we walk for our family, for our loved ones, and for the whole world.

SELF-CARE
WALKING WITH YOUR LOVED ONE

When you practice walking meditation, you can invite your loved one to walk with you. Imagine their hand in yours as you walk and feel their presence alive within you and beside you. When you walk with mindfulness, peace, and calm, your loved one is also walking mindfully, with peace and calm. When you stop to admire a beautiful view, to watch the setting sun, or listen to the birds singing, you can share this with your loved one. You look with their eyes.

You can ask them, "Dear ..., do you see this beautiful sunset? These beautiful trees?"

Enjoy everything for them. When you are fully mindful and in touch with your loved one and all your ancestors in the present moment, everyone benefits from and is nourished by the peace, joy, and the beauty of the moment. This is how we can heal ourselves and heal our loved ones and keep them alive within us.

MY MOTHER'S PRESENCE

Four years after my mother passed away, I had a dream in which I saw my mother—young, vivid, joyful and beautiful, with long black hair. Waking up at midnight, I went out to the moonlit garden. I experienced her presence as I walked on the hillside behind the temple. Each time my foot touched the ground, I felt her presence. And I knew my body was not mine alone but a long continuation of my mother and my father, my grandparents, and my ancestors. I discovered that my mother had never died. Together we were leaving footprints in the damp soil.

FOOTSTEPS IN THE SAND

Deserted beach,
Footsteps in the sand
Erased by rain—
This anguish comes from nowhere,
And its feet do not yet touch the Earth.

Suddenly I hear a far-off whisper
Of the gentle winds of Spring,
And the anguish is gone.

FREEDOM FROM DESPAIR

When we practice mindfulness, we touch freedom—freedom from remorse and regrets, freedom from anguish and fear. Freedom is the basis of happiness; without freedom, there can be no true happiness. Every step you make, every breath you take, every minute of sitting or walking meditation, and every action you take in mindfulness can bring you more peace, joy, solidity, and freedom.

HEALING THE
SUFFERING
OF SUICIDAL
THOUGHTS

There are teenagers and adults who don't know how to deal with their enormous suffering. They may think that the only way to get relief is to end their lives. Every day all over the world so many people of all ages kill themselves because they don't know how to handle their strong emotions.

We need to master the art of suffering ourselves so we can teach others this art, the art of transforming difficult emotions. We need to bring the practice of mindfulness into classrooms, into the workplace, and into our families. The practice of mindfulness, of stopping and looking deeply, and embracing our difficult feelings is very important. It can save lives.

YOUR LOVED ONE LIVES ON IN EVERYONE WHO KNEW THEM

We are our children and our children are us. If you have children, you have already been reborn in them. You can see your continuation body in your children very easily, but you have many more continuation bodies as well.

Everything your loved one has ever thought, said, or done is already being continued in those who know them. Everyone they have ever touched carries their continuation body. You cannot know how many people their words, thoughts, and actions have touched.

OUR TRUE LEGACY

Our actions of body, speech, and mind are our true legacy. This insight can liberate us from fear—our fear of being abandoned, of getting sick, and dying. We often try to forget that one day we, too, must die and will have to let go of everything we love. We cannot ignore this reality. We need to recognize our seed of fear and keep our awareness of impermanence alive every day.

You face the truth. You bring up the seed of fear within you, and you face it. You embrace it with your mindfulness and realize that the only thing that remains after you die are the consequences of your actions of body, speech, and mind. These are your true inheritance.

In my tradition, there are five remembrances we contemplate daily to remind ourselves of impermanence.

THE FIVE REMEMBRANCES

I am of the nature to grow old; there is no way to escape growing old.

I am of the nature to have ill health; there is no way to escape having ill-health.

I am of the nature to die; there is no way to escape death.

All that is dear to me and everyone I love are of the nature to change. There is no way to escape being separated from them.

I inherit the results of my actions of body, speech, and mind. My actions are my continuation.

SELF-CARE
COMMEMORATING YOUR
LOVED ONE

At a time when we may need strength, we can borrow from the strength of others. We can call on family and friends, but we can also call on our ancestors, spiritual teachers, and great beings to stand by us at this difficult time.

We do not need to wait until our loved one has died. As soon as we hear the news of a serious illness, we can meditate and send our energy of love, gratitude, and peace to that person. This kind of energy is healing and transformative.

If a number of close friends and family members or a group of fellow meditators can meditate with us, we can generate a powerful collective energy of mindfulness. This energy of prayer transcends time and space and can help not only we who are worried but also help the person who is ill or dying to feel more at peace.

○ ○ ○

In our tradition, we hold a ceremony of commemoration for the deceased as soon as they pass away and then at regular intervals—after seven days, forty-nine days, one hundred days, and then every year on the anniversary of their death. Of course, at first, we may be very sad, but such ceremonies do not need to be sad affairs. They are a chance for us to reconnect with our loved one, celebrate their life, and express our immense gratitude and love, as well as to offer them support on their journey of transformation and continuation.

○ ○ ○

We may like to hold a small ceremony at home, and invite family and friends to help create a strong collective energy. It can be helpful to do this as soon as possible after our loved one has died, so that we can offer prayers and send love and good wishes for a peaceful transition.

A ceremony can take many forms and can be as formal or as informal as you like. Before you start, you can prepare and offer your loved one their favorite food—something they really enjoyed eating or drinking while they were alive—and place it on the altar. You might like to place a card with their name and the dates of their birth and death beside their photo.

You can begin by lighting candles and offering incense, and practice sitting meditation for a short time to calm the body and mind and feel grounded. Then follow with a selection of chants, songs, readings, poems, or music.

We can recount special moments we had together and express our gratitude and appreciation for our loved one, and invite others to do the same. Hearing about the many ways that our loved one has touched the lives of others can bring us much joy.

The following contemplation is widely used in all our ceremonies for the deceased to remind us that we are much more than just this body and to remind us that, like a cloud, our loved one can be many things but can never die.

CONTEMPLATION ON NO COMING AND NO GOING

This body is not me.
I am not limited by this body.
I am life without boundaries.
I have never been born,
and I have never died.
Look at the ocean and the sky filled with stars,
manifestations from my wondrous True Mind.
Since before time, I have been free.
Birth and death are only doors through which we pass,
sacred thresholds on our journey.
Birth and death are a game of hide-and-seek.
So laugh with me,
hold my hand,
let us say good-bye,
say good-bye, to meet again soon.
We meet today.
We will meet again tomorrow.
We will meet at the source every moment.
We meet each other in all forms of life.

WE ARE LIKE FIREWORKS

When fireworks explode in the night sky,
sparks shoot out like flowers in all directions.
You are like fireworks. You do not continue in
a straight line; you radiate in all directions, into
your children, your friends, your society, and
the whole world.

When I share a teaching, it contains my
understanding of reality and my insights born
of experience, I am not going in a linear direc-
tion either. I am going out into you, and I am
being reborn in different forms in you and in
all the people who come in contact with this
teaching.

We do not need to wait until our body disintegrates to go on a journey of rebirth. At this
very moment we are being reborn in a multitude of different places and forms.

I AM NOT
IN HERE

I have a disciple in Vietnam who wants to build a stupa for my ashes when I die. He and others want to include a plaque with the words "Here lies my beloved teacher." I told them not to waste the temple land. "Do not put me in a small pot and put me in there!" I said. "I don't want to continue like that. It would be better to scatter the ashes outside to help the trees to grow."

I suggested that, if they still insisted on building a stupa, they have the plaque say, "I am not in here." But in case people don't get it, they could add a second plaque, "I am not out there either." If people still don't understand, then you can write on the third and last plaque, "I may be found in your way of breathing and walking."

This body of mine will disintegrate, but my actions will continue me. In my daily life, I always practice to see my continuation all around me. We don't need to wait until the total dissolution of this body to continue—we continue in every moment. If you think that I am only this body, then you have not truly seen me.

When you look at my friends, you see my continuation. When you see someone walking with mindfulness and compassion, you know they are my continuation. I don't understand why people say they are going to die because I can already see myself in you, in other people, and in future generations. I will never die. Every time I see one of my students walking in mindfulness, I see my continuation. There will be a dissolution of this body, but that does not mean my death. I will continue, always.

SELF-CARE
CULTIVATING GRATITUDE

Just as the practice of mindfulness can help us release sorrow, becoming aware of all the good conditions for happiness we already have can give us a more balanced view and help alleviate our suffering. When we look more closely, we see that we not only have pain and sorrow, but we also have many conditions for happiness which already exist. And there are a multitude of small moments of happiness that we can savor and add to each day. Can we recognize and appreciate them? Whether you drink a cup of tea, take a walk outside in nature, or just sit down quietly and look deeply, you can create happiness during that time. Recognizing the many small joys that life has to offer helps them grow, gladdens the mind, and brings us emotional relief.

° ° °

Take a piece of a paper and write down all the conditions for happiness available to you right now. Start with small, unspectacular things such as our own body and health. For example, "My heart is still beating and keeping me alive, even if my heart aches or is not as good as it once was." We usually take such things for granted but when we take a moment to focus on all the things that are good and still work well, it nourishes our gratitude and happiness and gladdens the mind.

Then, instead of focusing on our pain or regrets, we can begin to focus on the love and the good times we shared with our loved one, on all the wonderful memories we have of them.

You may be surprised to see that one page is not enough. Two pages may not be enough. Three or four pages may not be enough. When we recognize all the good conditions we already have, it's so easy to feel grateful, and gratitude is the foundation for happiness. With gratitude in our heart, we touch happiness and find relief from our suffering.

We can also make this a daily practice. Every night before going to bed, we can make a list of three things we are grateful for and one moment of happiness. Day by day, our gratitude and happiness will grow.

GRIEF AND COMPASSION: THE ART OF SUFFERING

We can learn a lot from our suffering. We can even speak of the *art* of suffering. When we know *how* to suffer, we suffer much less. We know that understanding our suffering gives rise to compassion, not only for ourselves, but also for others. And we know that compassion is essential for joy and happiness to be possible. We can learn to make good use of our suffering in order to grow our peace and happiness.

Many of us wonder what will happen to us when we die. Some of us think that after the dissolution of the body we rise up to heaven or float up to the clouds. Many believe we go to a distant paradise after we die which we imagine to be wonderful—a place without suffering.

But if heaven were a place with no suffering, I wouldn't want my children to go there. I wouldn't want to be in a world without any

155

suffering, because then there would be no com-passion or understanding either. If you haven't suffered hunger, you can't appreciate having something to eat. If you haven't gone through war, you don't know the value of peace.

We need to understand the goodness of suf-fering. It is the compost that helps the roses to grow. It is the mud from which magnificent lotuses emerge.

COMING BACK TO LIFE

We have a lamp inside us, the lamp of mindfulness, which we can light anytime. The oil of that lamp is our breathing, our steps, and our peaceful smile. We have to light up the lamp of mindfulness so the light will shine out all around and dissipate the darkness. Let's keep the lamp alight.

Whatever we do, we can do it in mindfulness, bringing our mind back to our body and the present moment. The present moment is our true refuge, our true home, the place where we can be fully alive. The past has already gone, and the future is not yet here. The present moment is the only moment we have to live. Let's do our best to enjoy it and not miss out on life.

SELF-CARE
A MORNING SMILE

Each morning when we wake up, we practice smiling. Being able to smile whether we feel like it or not is a deep practice in itself. "My suffering is not the end of the world," is what our smile says. Everything is impermanent, including our suffering. This, too, will pass. Research in neuroscience has shown that smiling sends a clear message to the brain that there is nothing to worry about, so smiling helps us feel better. We can welcome each new day with this awareness.

We may feel that smiling is the very last thing we can do right now, but waking up in the morning we become aware that we have a precious gift of twenty-four brand-new hours to live. We are still alive, and we want to make good use of the time given us. We do not want to waste it. We can live those twenty-four hours fully, and touch peace, joy, and wonder, despite the pain and suffering we may be experiencing. As we go through our day, we can generate the energy of understanding and compassion that has the capacity to heal us and everyone with whom we come into contact.

Reciting the following practice verse every morning before getting out of bed may help you start the day with more lightness and energy. You might like to write these words out and put them somewhere you can see them first thing in the morning.

Waking up this morning I smile.
Twenty-four brand-new hours are before me.
I vow to live fully in each moment
and to look at all beings
with the eyes of compassion.

The ocean of suffering is immense. But if you turn around, you can see the land.

The earth I tread this morning
transcends history.
Spring and Winter are both present in the moment.
The young leaf and the dead leaf are really one.
My feet touch deathlessness,
and my feet are yours.
Walk with me now.
Let us enter the dimension of oneness
and see the cherry tree blossom in Winter.
Why should we talk about death?
I don't need to die
to be back with you.

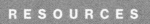

RESOURCES

BOOKS

Chan Khong, Sister. *Beginning Anew: Four Steps to Restoring Communication.* Berkeley, CA: Parallax Press, 2014.

Nhat Hanh, Thich. *The Art of Living: Peace and Freedom in the Here and Now.* New York: HarperCollins, 2017.

The Blooming of a Lotus: Revised Edition of the Classic Guided Meditation for Achieving the Miracle of Mindfulness. Boston: Beacon Press, 2009.

——. *Call Me by My True Names: The Collected Poems of Thich Nhat Hanh.* Berkeley, CA: Parallax Press, 1999.

——. *Chanting from the Heart: Buddhist Ceremonies and Daily Practices.* Berkeley, CA: Parallax Press, 2002.

——. *Happiness: Essential Mindfulness Practices.* Berkeley, CA: Parallax Press, 2005.

——. *Love Letter to the Earth.* Berkeley, CA: Parallax Press, 2012.

——. *Making Space: Creating a Home Meditation Practice.* Berkeley, CA: Parallax Press, 2011.

——. *The Miracle of Mindfulness.* Boston: Beacon Press, 1996.

——. *Peace of Mind: Becoming Fully Present.* Berkeley, CA: Parallax Press, 2013.

——. *Reconciliation: Healing the Inner Child.* Berkeley, CA: Parallax Press, 2006.

——. *Touching the Earth: 46 Guided Meditations for Mindfulness Practice.* Berkeley, CA: Parallax Press, 2003.

——. *Your True Home: The Everyday Wisdom of Thich Nhat Hanh.* Boulder, CO: Shambhala, 2011.

ONLINE RESOURCES

For retreats and guidance on applying the basic practices of mindfulness to our daily life, visit *plumvillage.org*.

For a wealth of resources—inspirational talks, guided meditations, deep relaxations, contemplations for touching the earth, and to download a mindfulness bell—visit *plumvillage.app*.

ABOUT THICH NHAT HANH

THICH NHAT HANH was a world-renowned spiritual teacher and peace activist. Born in Vietnam in 1926, he became a Zen Buddhist monk at the age of sixteen. Over seven decades of teaching, he published more than 100 books, which have sold more than four million copies in the United States alone. Exiled from Vietnam in 1966 for promoting peace, his teachings on Buddhism as a path to social and political transformation are responsible for bringing the mindfulness movement to Western culture. He established the international Plum Village Community of Engaged Buddhism in France, now the largest Buddhist monastery in Europe and the heart of a growing community of mindfulness practice centers around the world. He passed away in 2022 at the age of ninety-five at his root temple, Tu Hieu, in Hue, Vietnam.

Monastics and visitors practice the art of mindful living in the tradition of Thich Nhat Hanh at our mindfulness practice centers around the world. To reach any of these communities, or for information about how individuals, couples, and families can join in a retreat, please contact:

PLUM VILLAGE
33580 Dieulivol, France
plumvillage.org

LA MAISON DE L'INSPIR
77510 Villeneuve-sur-Bellot, France
maisondelinspir.org

HEALING SPRING
MONASTERY
77510 Verdelot, France
healingspringmonastery.org

MAGNOLIA GROVE
MONASTERY
Batesville, MS 38606, USA
magnoliagrovemonastery.org

BLUE CLIFF MONASTERY
Pine Bush, NY 12566, USA
bluecliffmonastery.org

DEER PARK MONASTERY
Escondido, CA 92026, USA
deerparkmonastery.org

EUROPEAN INSTITUTE OF
APPLIED BUDDHISM
D-51545 Waldbröl, Germany
eiab.eu

THAILAND PLUM VILLAGE
Nakhon Ratchasima
30130 Thailand
thaiplumvillage.org

ASIAN INSTITUTE OF
APPLIED BUDDHISM
Lantau Island, Hong Kong
pvfhk.org

STREAM ENTERING
MONASTERY
Beaufort, Victoria 3373
Australia
nhapluu.org

MOUNTAIN SPRING
MONASTERY
Bilpin, NSW 2758, Australia
mountainspringmonastery.org

For more information visit: *plumvillage.org*
To find an online sangha visit: *plumline.org*
For more resources, try the Plum Village app: *plumvillage.app*
Social media: *@thichnhathanh @plumvillagefrance*